Strategic Paper P3
Performance Strategy

First edition 2009

Fourth edition 2012

ISBN 9781 4453 9455 8 (previous edition ISBN 9780 7517 9592 9)

e-Book ISBN 9781 4453 9276 9

British Library Cataloguing-in-Publication Data

A catalogue record for this book is available from the British Library

Published by BPP Learning Media Ltd, BPP House, Aldine Place, London W12 8AA

www.bpp.com/learningmedia

Printed in the United Kingdom

Your learning materials, published by BPP Learning Media Ltd,
are printed on paper sourced from sustainable, managed forests.

Welcome to BPP Learning Media's CIMA **Passcards** for **Strategic Paper P3 Performance Strategy.**

- They **focus on your exam** and **save you time**.

- They incorporate **diagrams** to kick start your memory.

- They follow the overall **structure** of the BPP Learning Media Study Texts, but BPP Learning Media's CIMA **Passcards** are not just a condensed book. Each card has been separately designed for clear presentation. Topics are self contained and can be grasped visually.

- CIMA **Passcards** are still **just the right size** for pockets, briefcases and bags.

- CIMA **Passcards** should be used in conjunction with the revision plan in the front pages of the Kit. The plan identifies key questions for you to try in the Kit.

Run through the **Passcards** as often as you can during your final revision period. The day before the exam, try to go through the **Passcards** again! You will then be well on your way to passing your exams.

Good luck!

Contents

		Page
1	Introduction to risk	1
2	Risk management	7
3	Corporate governance	17
4	Ethics	25
5	Control systems I	31
6	Control systems II	43
7	Management accounting control systems	55
8	Financial risks	65

		Page
9	Interest rate risk	77
10	International risks	85
11	Transaction risk I	91
12	Transaction risk II	97
13	Information strategy and systems	109
14	Information operations	127
15	Internal audit	137
16	Internal audit review and reporting	145

1: Introduction to risk

Topic List

Nature of risks

Strategic risks

Operational risks

Types of risks

In this chapter we examine the main types of risk that organisations face and which you will encounter in exam scenarios. It emphasises the important distinction between strategic (long-term business) and operational (day-to-day) risks.

Risk

is a condition in which there exists a quantifiable dispersion in the possible outcomes from any activity. Risk can be classified in a number of ways.

Risk classification

Fundamental risks Affect society in general and cannot be controlled by one individual

Particular risks Risks over which individuals may have some control

Speculative risks Risks from which either good or harm may result

Pure risks Risks whose only possible outcome is harmful

Uncertainty

Uncertainty means possible outcomes and/or chances of each occurring are unknown.

Risk and return

Businesses/shareholders may tolerate higher risk levels provided they can receive a higher return.

Benefits of risk management

- Predictability of cash flows
- Well-run systems
- Limitation of impact of potentially bankrupting events
- Increased shareholder and investor confidence

Strategic risk

is the potential volatility of profits caused by the nature and type of business operations.

Strategic risks

Business risks **Non-business risks**

Competitor action   Product obsolescence   New technology   Finance   Accident/ disaster

Operational risk

is the risk of loss from a failure of internal business and control processes. It is also known as **process risk**.

Legal non-compliance	IT failure	Human error
⬆	⬆	⬆

Operational risks

⬇	⬇	⬇
Loss of key persons	Fraud	Business interruption

Competitor risks   Volatility of profits caused by actions of competitors

Product risks   Production of poor quality products resulting in customer compensation and loss of sales

Commodity risks   Shortage of supplies or large fluctuations in commodity prices

Stakeholder risks   Losses due to poor relations with stakeholders

Environmental risks   Risks from impact of environment or organisation's impact on environment

Financial risks   Possibility of loss or gain due to future changes in exchange or interest rates or market values

Legal risks   Risks of incurring legal penalties and costs

Political risks   Risk that political action will affect position and value

Cultural risks   Trading problems caused by different customs, laws and language

Technological risks	Computer malfunction, security breaches and technological progress making products obsolete
Knowledge management risks	Unauthorised use of intellectual property, loss of key information, staff departures
Property risks	Risks from damage, destruction or theft of property
Health and safety risks	Injuries to employees, loss of employee time, compensation
Trading risks	Physical, trade credit and liquidity risks
Cost/wastage risks	Incurring excessive supply costs or wasted employees' time
Fraud risks	Loss through fraudulent activities of staff or management
Reputation risks	Loss of reputation as result of adverse consequences of another risk

2: Risk management

Topic List

Risk management models

Risk appetite and culture

Risk assessment

Risk management

Risk responsibilities

Risk reporting

This chapter summarises the influences on the levels of risk that organisations accept, how they assess risk and what they do to manage it. Its contents are therefore very important for any question that may require you to recommend how to deal with risks or suggest a process to determine the risks they face.

Enterprise risk management (ERM)

is a process effected by the board of directors, management and other personnel, applied in strategy setting and across the enterprise, to identify potential events that may affect the entity and to manage risks to be within its risk appetite, and to provide reasonable assurance regarding the achievement of objectives.

ERM characteristics

- Process
- Operated at every level
- Applied in strategy setting
- Applied across enterprise

- Identifies key risks and manages the risk
- Provides reasonable assurance
- Geared to achievement of objectives

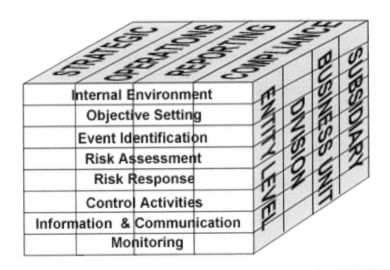

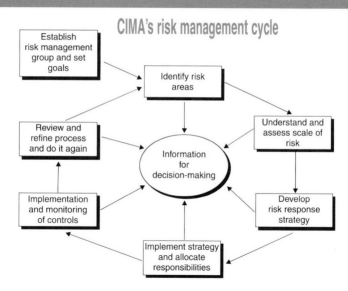

CIMA's risk management cycle

IFAC's Risk architecture

The risk architecture involves designing and implementing organisational structures, systems and processes to manage risk. It is slightly different to ERM.

Risk architecture components
■ Acceptance of a risk management framework
■ Commitment from executives
■ Establishment of a risk response strategy
■ Assignment of responsibility
■ Resourcing
■ Communication and training
■ Reinforcing risk cultures
■ Monitoring

IFAC's components of risk management

1 Structure

2 Resources

3 Culture

4 Tools and techniques

Shareholder demands

Personal views

Influences on risk appetite

Cultural influences

National influences

Organisational influences

Risk viewpoints

- Fatalists
- Hierarchists
- Individuals
- Egalitarians

Conformance and Performance

Conformance – Focus on controlling strategic risks by regulations, best practice, fiduciary responsibilities, efficient + effective risk management

Performance – Taking opportunities to increase returns, by alignment of strategy, value creation + resource utilisation

- Event identification
- Inspection of physical conditions/documents
- Enquiries and brainstorming
- Checklists
- Benchmarking
- Human reliability analysis

Identification

- Average results
- Frequency/chances of losses
- Largest possible loss

Analysis

Risk assessment

Mapping

Grouping risks into risk families, based on

- Frequency/likelihood
- Severity/consequences

Consolidation

- Aggregate of subsidiary risks for whole organisation

Dealing with risk

Abandonment	Not investing in high risk/high cost operations
Control	Contingency planning, physical measures (alarms, fire precautions) awareness and commitment
Acceptance	Bear full cost if risk materialises; valid if risks insignificant or avoidance costs too great
Transfer	To suppliers, customers, insurers, state
Sharing	With insurers/joint venture partners
Diversification	Portfolio management
Hedging	Incurring risks in opposite direction

Severity

Frequency	LOW	HIGH
LOW	Accept	Transfer
HIGH	Control or reduce	Abandon or avoid

Risk policy statement

Statement to be distributed to all managers and staff, covering

- Definitions
- Objectives
- Regulations
- Links with strategy
- Key risk management areas
- Key controls
- Roles of staff and managers

Risk register

- Lists and priorities main risks
- Those responsible for dealing with risks
- Actions taken and resulting risk levels

Risk management personnel

- Board
- Risk committee
- Risk managers/specialists
- Operational managers and staff
- Internal and external audit

Risk management function

- Set policy and strategy
- Build risk awareness and competence
- Establish risk management policy
- Design and review of processes
- Implement risk indicators and reports
- Prepare reports on risk

Board review

Boards need to consider:

- Nature and extent of significant risks taken
- Threat risks materialise
- Ability to reduce risk incidence/impact
- Costs and benefits of controls
- Frequency of monitoring

Monitoring

- Change identification/management
- Communication to right people
- Related to organisational size/complexity
- Formality

Internal risk reporting

Reporting needs to be:

- Comprehensive
- Regular
- Frequent for high impact-likelihood risks

Reporting needs to include:

- Comparisons actual v predicted risk
- Feedback on risk reduction
- Details of residual risk

External risk reporting

- Board responsibility
- Risk management process
- Review of effectiveness
- Impact of problems

3: Corporate governance

Topic List

Principles

Role of the board

Directors' remuneration

Reporting on internal control

Relationships

Corporate governance provides overall control over an organisation and monitors the specific controls that it operates. Corporate governance is a key area in the P3 syllabus and one of which you must have a good knowledge as it is frequently examined.

Corporate governance

is the system by which companies are directed and controlled.

Poor corporate governance	Governance principles
- Domination by single individual - Lack of board involvement - Lack of internal controls/audit - Poor supervision - No independent scrutiny - Little contact with shareholders - Short-term profits all important - Misleading accounts	- Adhere to strategic objectives - Minimise risk - Promote integrity - Fulfil responsibilities to stakeholders - Establish accountability - Maintain auditor/non-executive independence - Report accurately and promptly - Encourage shareholder involvement

Corporate governance reports

UK

- UK Corporate Governance Code
- Turnbull (internal control)
- Smith (audit committees)
- Higgs (non-executive directors)

USA

- Sarbanes - Oxley Act 2002

South Africa

- King

OECD

- Principles of corporate governance

Principles vs rules

A continuing debate on corporate governance is whether the guidance should predominantly be in the form of principles, or whether there is a detailed need for laws or regulations.

Directors' abilities and performance

- Relevant expertise
- Mix of experience/diversity on board
- Appropriate training
- Assess board performance at least once a year

Role of board

- Develop and ensure implementation of strategy
- Take major decisions (mergers, asset acquisitions, financing)
- Oversee chief executive
- Monitor risks and control systems
- Monitor human capital
- Oversee communication

Board membership

A nomination committee should oversee appointment process and make recommendations to the board, using objective criteria but attempting to recruit from a wide field.

Division of responsibilities

Effective power should not be vested in one person.

- Separation of chairman and chief executive
- Non-executive directors
- Senior independent director(s)

Chairman and Chief executive

Chairman runs board, responsible for shareholder communication and ensuring board has accurate data.

Chief executive oversees strategy, runs operations and control systems.

Non-executive directors (NEDs)

- No executive (managerial) responsibilities

- Provide balance

- Help reduce conflict

- Majority should be independent (no business/financial connection, no share options/pensions)

Role of NEDs

- Strategy
- Scrutiny
- Risk management
- Board personnel

NEDs

Advantages
- External experience and knowledge
- Wider perspective
- Comfort for investors
- Confidant/enabler
- Board members but objective

Disadvantages
- Independence?
- Restricted recruitment
- Difficult to impose views
- Can't prevent problems
- Limited time

Principles

UK guidance suggests:

- Directors' remuneration set by independent board members
- Bonuses/performance related pay related to measurable performance/enhanced shareholder value/long-term interests of company
- Full transparency in annual accounts

Remuneration committee

Committee of independent NEDs determining:

- Remuneration policy
- Specific remuneration packages

Should consider need to attract directors, interests of stakeholders, weighting and phasing of different parts of package including share options, performance measures.

Remuneration statement

Consider and disclose:

- Remuneration policy
- Arrangements for individual directors

Consider allowing members to vote on remuneration statement in accounts.

Service contracts

If service contracts are too long, premature termination may mean significant payments. Service contracts should not be > 12 months.

USA Sarbanes-Oxley

- Disclose deficiencies in internal control to auditors and audit committee
- Acknowledge responsibilities for internal control in accounts and assess effectiveness based on evaluation 30 days prior to report

UK Turnbull

The review of internal control should be an integral part of the company's operations.

London Stock Exchange

London Stock Exchange requires:

- Narrative statement of how principles of Code have been applied
- Statement of compliance/details of reasons for non-compliance

Major disclosures

- Board composition, directors, NED, evaluation of board performance
- Committee reports
- Relations with auditors and shareholders
- Business model/Financial strategy
- Review of internal controls
- Going concern
- Sustainability reporting

Relationships with shareholders

Directors should be held accountable by requiring them to submit to regular re-election (every three years). Boards should consider relationships with all shareholders, particularly institutional shareholders.

Hampel recommendations

- Send notice of AGM at least 20 working days before meeting
- Provide business presentation at AGM
- Question and answers sessions at AGM with committee chairman
- Shareholders vote separately on each substantially separate issue
- Shareholders vote on report and accounts

Relationships with stakeholders

OECD stresses role of:

- Employees
- Creditors
- Suppliers
- Shareholders
- Government

Position of stakeholders should be:

- Part of corporate governance
- Enhanced by participation (eg employees share ownership, profit-sharing arrangements)

4: Ethics

Topic List

CIMA's code of ethics

Company codes

Accountants in business

Approaching ethical problems

Ethical issues could frequently be brought into questions, particularly the role of control systems in enforcing them, or considering how auditors deal with ethical problems. Ethics are also important in the T4 exam.

Fundamental principles

CIMA's code emphasises the importance of students and members acting in the public interest. The objectives of the accountancy profession require members to produce credible information, show professionalism and deliver good quality services. The public must have confidence in the ethical framework.

Professional behaviour	Protects the reputations of the professional person and the professional body.
Integrity	Accountants must not be party to anything false or misleading.
Professional competence and due care	Perform services with reasonable care, competence and diligence
Confidentiality	No disclosure of confidential information without permission or legal or professional right or duty.
Objectivity	Avoid all bias, prejudice and partiality.

Ethical conflict

Guard against – often arises where loyalties are divided or pressure is applied.

T
H
R　　Advocacy
E
A　　Self-interest
T
S　　Intimidation

　　　Familiarity

　　　Self-review

Resolution of ethical conflicts

CIMA suggests:

- Gather all relevant information
- Raise concerns internally
- Raise concerns externally
- Remove self from situation

Professional safeguards

- Entry requirements
- CPD requirements
- Professional standards
- Laws/codes
- Resolution of ethical conflicts
- Professional monitoring
- Reporting requirements

Workplace safeguards

- Employer's oversight systems
- Employer's ethics and conduct programmes
- Ethical leadership
- HR/training procedures
- Communication/whistleblowing/consultation

Code of conduct

Code sets out expectations of ways employees will behave.

However, issuing a code isn't enough, the code needs to be backed by:

- Commitment of senior management
- Staff understanding of importance of ethics
- Staff commitment to ethics

Other measures

- Detailed guidance
- Identity and values stressed
- Training
- Reward schemes
- Whistle-blowing procedures
- Ethical departments/audits

Contents of codes

- Ethical principles
- Commitment required from employees
- Compliance with law
- Treatment of customers
- Treatment of suppliers
- Commitment to fair competition
- Commitment to environment
- Commitment to community
- Corporate citizenship

Problems with codes

Codes may be seen as inflexible and unfair sets of rules, that are not relevant to the ethical situations employees encounter.

Professional and employment obligations

Accountants should fulfil legal and ethical obligations, including confidentiality. However accountants may be pressurised to act illegally or unethically, including being responsible for misleading information.

Preparation and reporting of information

Information should describe clearly nature of business transactions, classify and record information in timely and proper manner, and represent facts accurately.

Acting with expertise

Competent performance by accountant may be threatened by lack of time, lack of information, insufficient training, inadequate resources.

Financial interests

Share ownership, share options and profit-related bonuses provide incentives to manipulate information. Disclosure of relevant information counters this threat.

Inducements

Accountants may appear to be compromised by having being offered an inducement as well as accepting one. Accountants need to disclose offer to senior management, also to third parties.

How to gain marks

Marks will be awarded for:

- Analysis of the situation

- Recognition of ethical issues

- Explanations of relevant ethical guidance

- Making clear, logical and appropriate recommendations

- Justifying recommendations in practical business and ethical terms

Step-by-step approach

1 Identify key facts

2 Identify ethical issues and fundamenal principles

3 Consider alternative actions and consequences

4 Recommend action

5 Justify decision

5: Control systems I

Topic List

Systems

Control systems

Contingency theory

Structure of organisations

Organisational culture

Human resources

In this chapter we examine control systems.

We also look at the way organisations can be structured and the different cultures that can be put in place. The chapter ends with a consideration of how organisation can be controlled by human resource policies.

A system has three component parts: INPUTS, PROCESSES and OUTPUTS. The environment and system boundary are also key characteristics.

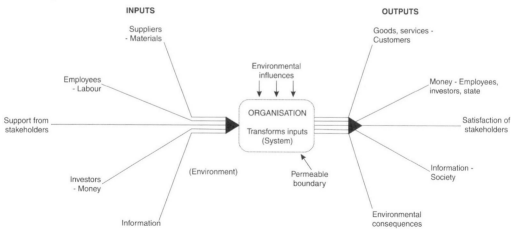

INPUTS

Suppliers
- Materials

Employees
- Labour

Support from stakeholders

Investors
- Money

Information

Environmental influences

ORGANISATION

Transforms inputs
(System)

(Environment)

Permeable boundary

OUTPUTS

Goods, services -
Customers

Money - Employees,
investors, state

Satisfaction of stakeholders

Information -
Society

Environmental consequences

Subsystems

Systems may contain subsystems with their own objectives. Separate subsystems interact and respond. Goals of subsystems must be consistent with goals of overall system.

Subsystems can be differentiated by function, space, time, formality, people and organisation.

Closed systems

Closed systems are isolated from, and independent of, their environment.

Open systems

Open systems are influenced by their environment and influence environment by their behaviour. Influences may have predictable consequences.

Open systems
■ Link technical and social aspects of organisations
■ Focus on links between individuals and subsystems and rest of organisation
■ Stress significance of boundaries round subsystems and systems, relations across boundaries and boundary management

Components of systems

Objectives	Targets at which organisation is aiming
Sensor	Device/person by which data is collected and measured
Operations	Inputs, processes and outputs
Comparator	Means by which actual results measured against plans/system objectives
Effector	Device/means by which control action is initiated

Loop systems

In loop systems, part of the output is fed back to the system (**feedback**). Feedback is used to control the behaviour of the system.

Feedback control

The measurement of differences between planned output and outputs achieved, and modification of subsequent action/plans to produce required results.

Positive feedback

Positive feedback leads to control action that causes actual results to maintain/increase deviation away from planned results

Negative feedback

Negative feedback results in corrective action that seeks to bring results or activities back towards planned course or targets

Feedforward control

The forecasting of differences between actual and planned outcomes, and the implementation of action before the event, to avoid differences.

Feedback/feedforward control problems

- Uncertainty in predicting environment
- Unpredictable behaviour of individuals
- Preparing reliable plans
- Measuring results with accuracy and in suitable time
- Identifying causes and controllability of variations
- Persuading managers to take action
- Co-ordinating and circulating feedback
- Changing plan/comparator/effector – this will require **double loop** feedback rather than **single loop** actual: planned comparison

S tructure of organisation

E nvironmental conditions

C ulture

R ole of centre

E stablished strategy

T echnology use and dependency

| Systems | Control systems | Contingency theory | **Structure of organisations** | Organisational culture | Human resources |

Components of organisation

Strategic apex	Directors
Operating core	People involved in process of adding value
Middle line	Middle managers, link between strategic centre and operating core
Techno structure	Finance dept, HRM, designers of controls
Support staff	Marketing, IT, legal, financial

Tall and flat organisations

Tall organisations have a lot of management layers, too rigid and block initiative

Flat organisations have relatively few levels, allow delegation and empowerment

Empowerment

- Work teams achieve / set targets
- Delayering of command chain
- Flexibility to serve customer needs
- Encourages knowledge workers + new IT

Hierarchies

Organisation's hierarchy embodies relationships of responsibility, direction and control.

Influences on structure

- Age (greater formality if older)
- Size (if big, more elaborate structure, bigger units, greater formality)
- Information technology
- Dynamism of environment (more fluid if high)
- Complexity of environment (decentralisation)
- External hostility/control (centralisation)
- Power needs (centralisation)

Centralisation and decentralisation

Degree to which authority is delegated.

Centralisation

- Decisions centrally co-ordinated
- Easier for central managers to devise strategy and keep balance
- Better quality strategic decision making
- Enables standardisation

Decentralisation

- Avoids overburdening central management
- Improved local motivation
- Greater awareness of local problems
- Better quality operational/tactical decision making
- Enables local managers to develop

Functional organisation

Departments defined by functions (the work they do).

Advantages

- Logical
- Economies of scale

Disadvantages

- Doesn't reflect value creation
- Lack of whole business view
- Lack of co-ordination

Matrix organisation

Dual command structure, perhaps management by product as well as by function. Subordinates have two or more superiors.

Advantages

- Flexibility
- Improved communication/co-operation
- Multiple orientation

Disadvantages

- Conflicts between managers
- Greater stress for individuals
- Complex

Divisionalisation

Divisions are strategic business units with local autonomy. They can be constructed on the basis of geography, product, customers or technology.

Outsourcing

Outsourcing is use of external suppliers to supply products or services.

- Frees up internal time and resources
- Makes specialist expertise available
- Cost – effectiveness
- Needs monitoring of quality of services
- Staff unhappiness/ loss of skills
- Transfer of sensitive data

Business process re-engineering

A reorganisation of the organisation's activities in response to the demands of the business environment.

- Radical changes to ways of doing business
- Changing structures in response to customer requirements
- Address lack of staff accountability

Horizontal organisation

Organisation structure based on cross-functional process:

- Team-focused
- Process ownership
- Customer drives process

Culture

is the sum total of the beliefs, knowledge, attitudes of mind and customs to which people are exposed, including the assumptions they use to deal with situations.

Cultural control

Cultural control is control through shared values and mission, but allowing maximum individual autonomy and expression.

Handy's cultures

Power

All communication, decisions and control channelled through a single source, dependent on key individuals

Role/bureaucracy

Formal, well established rules and procedures, detailed job descriptions

Task

Matrix organisation, using project teams/task forces. Getting jobs done is paramount

Person

Serves interests of individuals within organisation

5: Control systems I

Human resource management (HRM)

Coherent and strategic approach to managing the organisation's most valuable assets, the people working there.

Control techniques include recruitment and selection, contracts of employment, role definition, training and appraisals.

Management performance measures

- Subjective ranking, measures
- Outsider judgements
- Upward appraisal
- Tailored accounting measures
- Non-financial measures such as market share

Behaviour control

- How work performed
- Sequence of tasks
- Used when difficult to assess outcomes
- Legal requirements
- Risk avoidance

Output control

- Sales/profitability level
- Service delivery
- Operational standards
- Performance targets

6: Control systems II

Topic List

Internal control frameworks

Communication of control

Control environment

Control procedures

Fraud

Control self assessment

This chapter emphasises the importance not only of having an appropriate control structure in place, but also communication of the aims of controls to employees.

This chapter also looks at how the risk of fraud is mitigated through the use of appropriate controls.

The chapter ends with an examination of control self assessment as a tool for senior management to assess internal control.

Internal control is any action taken by management to enhance the likelihood that established objectives and goals will be achieved.

CONTROL FRAMEWORK

Control environment

Control procedures

Aims of controls

Controls are designed to achieve the following aims:

- Appropriate response to risks (safeguarding of assets, liability management)
- Ensure quality of reporting (maintenance of records, generation of relevant information)
- Ensure compliance with laws and regulations

COSO and **COCO** are commonly used control frameworks.

Limitations of controls

Internal controls reduce but don't eliminate risk of:

- Losses through bad decisions
- Human error
- Circumvention of controls
- Management override
- Unforeseeable circumstances

Communication of policies

Turnbull report recommends policies are communicated in following areas:

- Customer relations
- Service levels
- Health, safety and environment
- Asset security and business continuity
- Expenditure
- Accounting, financial and other reporting

Communication methods

- Guidance from chief executive
- Circulation of risk policies
- Staff involvement in policy development
- Workshops and training
- Whistleblowing procedures

Human resource issues

Turnbull stresses that employees need skills, knowledge and understanding in relation to risks organisation faces.

Aims of HR

- Remuneration policies/working policies encourage responsible behaviour
- 'Right first time' culture
- Ensure everyone is aware of responsibilities
- Encourage reporting of problems
- Co-ordination of activities
- Common risk management vocabulary across organisation
- Adoption of working practices and training that result in better performance

Control environment

The overall attitude, awareness and actions of directors and management regarding internal controls and their importance in the entity.

Control environment factors

- Management's philosophy and operating style
- Culture
- Organisational structure
- Methods of imposing control
- Integrity, ethical values and competence

Strong control environment

- Clear risk management strategies
- Culture/code of conduct/HRM/reward systems support objectives and risk limitation
- Senior management commitment to competence, integrity and trust
- Clear authority and responsibility
- Communication procedures
- Staff have knowledge, skills and tools

Classification of controls

Prevent	Stop errors happening including checks of documentation before payment/deliveries made
Detect	Pick up errors such as reconciliations and physical counts
Correct	Minimise or negate errors eg back-up
Direct	Send activities/staff to desired outcome, eg manuals, training
Financial	Accounting records, budgets, investment appraisal
Non-financial quantitative/ qualitative	Balanced scorecard, TQM, strategic plans, HRM, governance
Input	Resources used
Process	Operational activities
Output	Products or services produced

Types of control procedures

- Segregation of duties
- Physical
- Authorisation of transactions
- Management review of information
- Supervision
- Organisational structure
- Arithmetic (reconciliations)
- Personnel
- Information systems
- Internal audit
- Audit committee

Accounting system controls

Risks	**Control aims**
■ Failure to receive income	■ Income received fully
■ Asset misappropriation (cash, inventory, non-current assets)	■ Assets safeguarded against pilferage
■ Deterioration in asset value	■ Assets safeguarded against damage
■ Unauthorised transactions	■ Transactions authorised and completed
■ Purchases not giving value for money	■ Value received for monies paid
■ Deterioration in customer relationships	■ Dealings with customers on agreed terms
■ Deterioration in supplier relationships	■ Dealings with suppliers on agreed terms
■ Failure to record accounting items	■ Assets, liabilities, transactions recorded correctly

Segregation of duties

Full documentation

Information comparison/ completeness

Physical security

Key accounting system controls

Authorisation

Asset review

Reperformance

External confirmation

Operational controls

Risks	Control aims
■ Assets/resources not available when required	■ Assets/resources available for business use
■ Assets/resources/staff not used efficiently	■ Assets/resources/staff used most efficiently
■ Facilities not available when required	■ Facilities can be used
■ Loss of sales due to operational problems	■ Identification of customer requirements
■ Damage to assets	■ Assets protected against damage
■ Misappropriation of assets	■ Assets secured against loss
■ Interruption of business	■ Back-up resources available
■ Failure to comply with internal guidelines	■ Internal guidelines meet risks and are followed
■ Failure to comply with external legislation	■ Procedures ensure compliance with laws

Resource review

Asset review

Quality control

Supplier review/
tendering

Key operational controls

Planning/
forecasting

Variance
analysis

Reports to
management

Asset security
procedures

Contingency
plans/facilities

Types of fraud

1 Ghost employees

2 Miscasting of payroll

3 Stealing unclaimed wages

4 Collusion with external parties

5 Altering cheques and inflating expenses claims

6 Stealing assets

7 Identity fraud

8 Issuing false credit notes

9 Sales fraud

Fraud risks

- Integrity of management
- Financial reporting pressures
- Weaknesses in internal control systems
- Unusual transactions or trends
- Problems in obtaining audit evidence

Fraud conditions

- Dishonesty
- Opportunity
- Motive

Prevention of fraud

This must be an integral part of corporate strategy.

Fraud prevention	
General policies	*Specific business areas*
■ Emphasising ethics	■ Segregation of duties
■ Personnel controls	■ Appropriate documentation
■ Training and raising awareness	■ Limitation controls
■ Disciplinary procedures	■ Actions prohibited
	■ Internal audit work

Detection of fraud

Staff must be aware of their responsibilities. Information must also be available to allow management to identify signs of fraud.

Investigation of fraud

1 Establish extent of loss

2 Establish how fraud occurred

3 Consider individuals implicated

4 Assess controls in place

Control self assessment

Control self assessment is assessment by senior managers with support of internal audit on the adequacy of internal controls throughout the organisation

Risk analysis 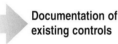 **Documentation of existing controls** **Assessment of existing control** **Reporting and review across whole organisation**

Managers' information requirements

Managers need information about:

- Risks linked to achievement of organisation's objectives
- Control mechanisms responding to changes in environment

Manager action

- Compare different data sources
- Consider adequacy of communication channels
- Provide feedback
- Review information systems

7: Management accounting control systems

Topic List

Risks of management accounting systems

Management accounting systems

Budgeting

Management accounting problems

Developments in systems

Management accounting function

This chapter focuses on the key influences on, and elements of, management accounting control systems. You may be asked about the impact of strategic decisions on management accounting systems and measures, and on financial, non-financial quantitative and qualitative controls.

Elements of management accounting systems

Simons identified the need for management accounting systems to be useful for score-keeping, attention-directing and problem-solving. They should assist strategic planning, management control and operational control.

Problems with traditional systems

Recent developments that give traditional systems problems:

- Globalisation and increased competition
- Information technology and data flows
- Reorganisations and mergers

Risks of management accounting systems

1 Excessive emphasis on financial measures

2 Internal orientation

3 Lack of goal congruence

4 Lack of future perspective

5 Failure to adopt the right performance measures

Strategic management accounting

Stresses factors relating to external parties, customers, competitors. **Forward looking** and concerned with **values**.

Designing a system

- Sources of input and whether sources can deliver required information
- Processing
- Output required based on information needs
- Different types of information (strategic planning, management and operational control)
- Response dependent on detail and how information is presented
- When required

Manufacturing sector performance

- Quality
- Reliability
- Process time
- Flexibility

Service sector performance

- Flexibility
- Innovation
- Resource utilisation
- Excellence
- Financial performance
- Competitiveness

7: Management accounting control systems

Budget decisions

There are a number of decisions that have to be made in relation to how budgets are prepared:

- Budget centres may be chosen on basis of activities, functions, products, areas, customers
- Focus may be costs, revenues, profit, ROI
- Whether to establish service centres as profit centres, focusing on volume and value of services
- How much managers participate
- Use of beyond budgeting performance targets

Problems with budgeting

- Budgets seen as pressure device
- Budgets of different departments conflict
- Budgetary slack
- Unachievable budgets set
- Efforts limited to achieving targets
- Encourages rigidity
- Excessive concentration on short-term
- Too hard or too soft targets demotivate

Low-level budgeting

Advantages

- Motivates junior managers
- Better awareness of management responsibilities
- Better awareness of detail

Disadvantages

- Acts against centralisation
- Managers work in own interests
- More budget centres, more complexity
- Greater opportunity for budgetary slack

Timing
: Management accountants focus on the production stage, not the design stage when the key decisions are made.

Controllability
: Focus is on direct costs, rather than overheads, when overheads are more difficult to control.

Different assets
: Systems have difficulty measuring non-tangible assets and how they affect resource allocation and strategic value.

Customers
: Systems fail to analyse how customers drive costs.

Cost reporting
: Reporting reflects functional structure rather than processes that drive costs and cut across functions.

Absorption costing
: Absorption rates based on labour hours are inappropriate for many modern non-labour intensive processes. Activity-based costing may be a better method.

Standard costing	Inappropriate where flexibility/customisation/service are important.
Short-term financial measures	Take too long to produce/too narrow.
Cost accounting methods	Emphasis on quantifiable financial benefits at expense of non-quantifiable or non-financial benefits.
Variances	Can produce inappropriate responses (excess inventory).
Investment appraisal	Fail to consider financial constraints/strategic issues.
Transfer pricing	Problems resolving conflict between economic price and inappropriate behaviour transfer price may encourage.
Balanced scorecard	Range of measures, links with strategy, but difficult to understand/gain overall impression.
Environmental reporting	Full cost accounting including hidden costs, contingent liabilities, rectification costs.

7: Management accounting control systems

Just in time/Total Quality Management

Both emphasise commitment to continuous improvement. JIT involves search for excellence in design + operation of production management. TQM applies zero defects philosophy to management of all resources and relationships, and focuses on customers.

Life cycle costing

Majority of product's life cycle costs committed at early stages of cycle and hence highest cost controls are required at this stage.

Focus on planning and control of life cycle, and spending commitments in early years.

Throughput accounting

Identification and elimination of bottleneck resources by overtime, product changes and process alterations to reduce set-up and waiting times.

Lean management accounting

Lean management accounting aims to support production flow based on customer demand. It is designed to encourage continuous quality improvement and the elimination of waste. It uses management through value streams and target costing to eliminate distortions that result in non-optimal behaviour.

Target costing

Product is developed, managers determine market selling price and desired profit margin. Cost of production is therefore the balancing figure which must be achieved.

Kaizen

Kaizen is applied during the production process. It focuses on key elements of operations, production, purchasing and distribution. Aims to achieve a specified cost reduction through continuous improvements, rather than one-off changes.

Transaction cost economics

Relevant for determining transfer prices. Focuses on costs such as negotiation, administration, time commitments and obligations.

Backflush costing

Can significantly reduce detailed work done by accounting department. Costs calculated and charged when product sold or when transferred to finished goods store.

7: Management accounting control systems

Management accounting function

Provides information aiding planning, control and decision – making, resource usage and asset security.

Increasing emphasis on linking different sources of information, and providing information tailored to particular decisions, such as risk management.

Measurement of management accounting function

- User satisfaction surveys/complaints
- Delivery of information on time
- Benchmarking v functions in other organisations/external providers
- Speed of query response
- Number of ad hoc reports

Objectives

- Provision of good information
- Provision of value for money service
- Availability of informed personnel
- Flexibility

8: Financial risks

Topic List

Financial risks

Risk quantification methods

Using the results

Treasury function

Risk management

Accounting requirements

This chapter recaps the key financial risks. It also covers how these financial risks are measured and managed.

Financing/Liquidity

Foreign investment/trading

Credit

Financial risks

Fraud

Market

Accounting

Sensitivity analysis

Sensitivity analysis is a modelling and risk assessment process in which changes are made to significant variables in order to determine the effect of these changes on the outcome. Particular attention is then paid to variables identified as being of special significance.

Example

NPV of a project with an initial investment of £500,000 is £80,000. The initial investment can rise by $(80,000/500,000) \times 100\% = 16\%$ before the investment just breaks even.

Key variables

- Selling price
- Sales volume
- Cost of capital
- Initial cost
- Operating costs
- Benefits

Weaknesses

- Difficult to analyse interdependencies
- Change in more than one variable can't be calculated this way
- No indication of likelihood
- May be difficult to control critical factors
- Managers decide what is acceptable

Certainty equivalent approach

The certainty equivalent approach involves converting expected cash flows into equivalent risk-free amounts and discounting at the risk-free rate. The greater the risk of the expected cash flow:

- The smaller the certainty equivalent receipt
- The larger the certainty equivalent payment

Disadvantages of certainty equivalents

- Adjustments to cash flows decided subjectively
- Ascertaining the risk-free rate

Expected values (EV)

The EV of an opportunity is equal to the sum of (the probability of an outcome occurring (p) × return expected if it does occur (x)) = Σpx.

The calculation of EVs is more useful when outcomes occur many times over.

Expected values and NPV

1. Calculate NPV

2. Measure risk:

   - Worst outcome and probability
   - Probability negative result
   - Standard deviation of NPV

Regression analysis

Measures sensitivity of cash flows to various risk factors.

Simulations

Used to assess projects with lots of outcomes, or projects with correlated cash flows.

Scenarios

Used as a means of predicting alternative situations based on changing conditions. They can be used to quantify possible losses and as a basis for developing **contingency plans**.

Value at risk (VAR)

> Mean – (confidence interval value for X% × standard deviation)

Example

Possible gains or losses on daily trading normally distributed around mean of 0 + daily standard deviation of £10,000. Daily VAR at 5% confidence is

1 Daily volatility - £10,000

2 Normal value 95(100 – 5)% = 1.65

3 VAR = 1.65 x 10,000 = £16,500

5% chance daily loss > £16,500

Investment appraisal

Maximum payback period	Reflecting increased risks of long-term cash flows
High discounting rate	Reflecting increased risks of long-term cash flows
Selection of low risk projects	Those with low standard deviations and acceptable predicted outcomes
Focus on critical decision-making factors	As determined by sensitivity analysis
Use pessimistic estimates/estimates with slack	Ensure future no worse than predicted

Budgeting

Modelling financial risks	Preparing different budgets with different assumptions
Considering risks	Subjecting current budget to probability/sensitivity analysis

Treasury management

The corporate handling of financial matters, the generation of external and internal funds for the business, the management of currencies and cash flows and the complex strategies, policies and procedures of corporate finance.

Treasury risks

- Lack of funds curtailing business
- Hedging resulting in losses
- Failure to communicate exposures
- Lack of flexibility to local needs
- Difficulties in exercising control

Treasury policy statement

The statement should cover the treasury function's roles and responsibilities, risks requiring management, authorisation and dealing limits.

Treasury audit

Auditors should confirm that risks are managed in accordance with company procedures and the board is kept informed.

Other controls

- Forecasts
- Defined risk tolerances
- Contingency arrangements
- Investment reviews

- Debt/equity mix
- International

Diversification

- Natural hedging
- Internal netting
- Working capital management

Internal strategies

Financial risk management

Risk sharing

- Forwards
- Futures
- Joint ventures
- Swaps

Risk transfer

- Options
- Insurance
- Securitisation

8: Financial risks

Disclosures are determined by IAS 32 and 39 and IFRS 7 and 9

Categorisation

Main provisions are:

- Classify as financial liability, financial asset or equity
- Critical feature is incurring contractual obligation to deliver cash
- Treatment of interest/dividends depends on whether relate to financial instruments or equity

Categories

- Financial asset/liability held at fair value
- Held to maturity investments
- Loans and receivables
- Available for sale financial assets

Measurement

Main requirements are:

- Financial assets measured at fair value or amortised cost
- If measured at fair value, gains and losses in profit or loss
- If measured at amortised cost, interest included in profit or loss
- Financial liabilities mostly at amortised cost
- Fair value: quoted market price or other valuation techniques

Hedging

Hedging means designating one or more hedging instruments so that change in fair value is offset by change in fair value or cash flows of hedged items.

- **Fair value** hedges – recognise in profit or loss
- **Cash flow** hedges – recognise effective portion in other comprehensive income
- Disclose hedges + risks being hedged

Risk disclosures

- Exposures to risk
- Objectives, policies + processes for managing risk
- Changes in exposure/management
- Summary quantitative data

Processes and systems

Compliance with IASs will impact on systems.

- Processing of transactions
- Internal and external communication
- Risk management techniques
- Limits to activities
- Monitoring

Organisational aims

- Value assets, liabilities, derivatives
- Produce documentation of hedging strategies
- Provide testing of effectiveness
- Managing hedging relationships
- Generate necessary information
- Accomodate IAS requirements

9: Interest rate risk

Topic List

Interest rate risk

FRAs and pooling

Interest rate futures

Interest rate options

Interest rate swaps

In this chapter we examine interest rate risk and some of the financial instruments that can be used to manage financial risks, such as derivatives.

You may be asked to consider a range of options to counter interest rate risk.

Sources of risk

1 Fixed v floating rate debt

2 Currency of debt

3 Term of loan

4 Term loan v overdraft

Interest rate risk management

- Netting
- Smoothing
- Matching
- Pooling
- Forward rate agreements
- Interest rate futures
- Interest rate options or guarantees
- Interest rate swaps

Interest rate risk is often not hedged because of the costs, lack of availability of appropriate instruments, remoteness of risk crystallising or immateriality of impact if the risk does crystallise.

Forward rate agreement (FRA)

is an agreement, typically between a company and a bank, to fix the interest rate charged/received on future borrowing or bank deposits.

A 3-9 FRA starts in three months and lasts for six months.

FRAs	
Advantages	*Disadvantages*
■ Protection provided	■ Rate > current market
■ Flexibility on time and size	■ Falling interest rate
■ Low cost	■ FRAs expire and need to be renegotiated
	■ No market for these

Netting

Aggregating and hedging net exposure.

Smoothing

Maintaining a balance between fixed and floating rate borrowing.

Matching

Matching assets and liabilities that have a common interest rate.

Pooling

If organisation has different accounts with same bank, pooling balances for interest charges and overdraft limits.

Interest rate futures

Interest rate futures hedge against interest rate movements. The terms, amounts and periods are standardised:

- The futures prices will vary with changes in interest rates
- Outlay to buy futures is less than buying the financial instrument
- Price of short-term futures quoted at discount to 100 Par value (93.40 indicates deposit trading at 6.6%)

Interest rate futures	
Advantages	*Disadvantages*
■ Cost	■ Inflexibility of terms
■ Amount hedged	■ Basis risk
■ Traded so can be sold on	■ Daily settlement

Interest rate option

grants the buyer the right, but not the obligation, to deal at an agreed interest rate at a future maturity date.

If a company wishes to hedge **borrowing, purchase put options**.

If a company wishes to hedge **lending, purchase call options**.

Strike price	Puts			Calls		
	Nov	Dec	Jan	Nov	Dec	Jan
113.50	0.87	1.27	1.34	0.29	0.69	1.06

- Strike price is price paid for futures contract
- Numbers under each month represent premium paid for option contract
- Put options more expensive than call as interest rates predicted to rise

Valuation of options

Black-Scholes model measures impact of factors affecting value:

- Current value
- Exercise price
- Time to expiry
- Variability of share price
- Risk-free rate of return

| Interest rate risk | FRAs and pooling | Interest rate futures | **Interest rate options** | Interest rate swaps |

Interest rate cap sets an interest rate ceiling. **Interest rate floor** sets lower limit to interest rates.

Interest rate collar means can buy interest rate cap and sell floor. Zero-cost collar is when premium for buying cap equals premium for selling floor.

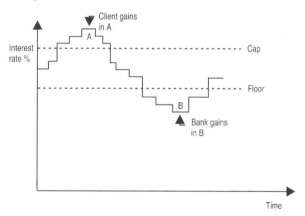

Interest rate swaps

are transactions that exploit different interest rates in different markets for borrowing, to reduce interest costs for either fixed or floating rate loans.

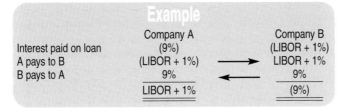

Example

	Company A	Company B
Interest paid on loan	(9%)	(LIBOR + 1%)
A pays to B	(LIBOR + 1%) ⟶	LIBOR + 1%
B pays to A	9% ⟵	9%
	LIBOR + 1%	(9%)

Advantages

- Flexibility and costs
- Use of credit ratings
- Capital restructuring
- Risk management
- Easy to arrange
- Predictability of cash flows

Disadvantages

- Counterparty risk
- Become subject to floating interest rates
- Lack of liquid market
- Costs/time not worth benefits

Uses of interest rate swaps

- Switching from paying one type of interest to another
- Raising less expensive loans
- Securing better deposit rates
- Managing interest rate risk
- Avoiding charges for loan termination

10: International risks

Topic List

International risks

Economic and translation risks

Political risks

Product and cultural risks

Trading and credit risks

This chapter covers the risks faced by businesses that have international investments. Such risks include adverse movements in exchange rates and political and cultural risks.

International risks

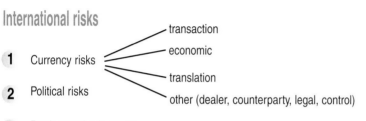

1. Currency risks
   - transaction
   - economic
   - translation
   - other (dealer, counterparty, legal, control)

2. Political risks

3. Product and culture risks

4. Trading and credit risks

Control of international risks

A business can reduce its exposure to international risks by diversification of its trading interests or portfolio of investments.

Economic exposure

is the risk that exchange rate movements might reduce the international competitiveness of a company.

Translation exposure

is the risk that the organisation will make exchange losses when the accounting results and position of its foreign branches or subsidiaries are translated into home currency.

Controlling economic exposure

- Matching assets and liabilities
- Diversifying supplier and customer base
- Diversifying operations worldwide

Translation exposure probably does not need to be hedged. Sometimes it may be hedged if a business believes that investors will be unhappy with translation losses.

Political risks

Political risks can arise through various forms of government actions, such as:

- Quotas, limiting quantities
- Tariffs, making imports more expensive
- Legal standards
- Restrictions on foreign ownership
- Nationalisation

Controlling political risks

- Negotiate concessions
- Insurance
- Production strategies
- Maintain contact with markets
- Financial management
- Threaten withdrawal

Blocked funds

Blocked funds arise from restrictions on types of transaction for which payments abroad allowed, such as bans on dividends to overseas shareholders.

Controlling blocked funds

- Sales of goods and services to subsidiary
- Royalty charges
- Interest on loans
- Management charges

Legal risks

The risks of problems with legal systems including:

- Suffering penalties due to non-compliance with laws
- Expending resources to ensure compliance
- Suffering losses through inability to enforce legal rights (such as copyright)

Dealing with legal risks

- Legal action (costly)
- Relocation of operations to where legal burden is lower
- Ensure awareness of relevant regulations
- Lobby for/to prevent changes
- Act as good citizen, complying with voluntary codes

Cultural risks

Cultural risks are the risks of suffering disruption through problems with overseas staff, or the risk of losing business overseas through failing to understand local practices and ways of doing business.

Dealing with cultural risks

- Enter markets where culture is compatible
- Adapt products to local conditions
- Use appropriate control systems (centralisation/decentralisation balance)
- Use of expatriate staff (consider cost, failure of expatriates to adjust to local culture)
- Give local staff opportunities/appropriate training

Foreign trade

Foreign trade has various features that may mean payment is delayed, including extended credit, time needed to arrange exports, paperwork and transport time.

Physical risk	The risk of goods or documentation being lost or stolen in-transit
Credit risk	Possibility of payment default by customer
Trade risk	The risk of the customer refusing to accept the goods or the cancellation of the order
Liquidity risk	Inability to finance the credit

Controlling credit risk

- Export factoring
- Forfaiting
- Documentary credits
- International credit unions
- Export credit insurance
- Acceptance credits
- Export merchants
- Government departments

11: Transaction risk I

Topic List

Exchange rates

Transaction risks

Forward exchange contracts

Money market hedging

Do not neglect the topics in this chapter in favour of the more technically complex subjects in Chapter 12. Exam questions may cover the whole range of options available to a company, and contain discussion elements as well as calculations.

Direct quote is amount of domestic currency equal to one foreign currency unit.

Indirect quote is amount of foreign currency equal to one domestic unit.

Influences on exchange rates

- Interest rates
- Inflation rates
- Balance of payments
- Market sentiment/speculation
- Government policy

Remember!

Company sells	base currency	LOW
buys	base currency	HIGH

For example, if UK company is buying and selling pounds, selling (offer) price may be 1.45 $ per £, buying (bid) price may be 1.47 $ per £.

Remember!

If the exchange rate is Home 1 unit = Foreign X units DIVIDE foreign currency amount by rate.

If the exchange rate is Foreign 1 unit = Home X units MULTIPLY foreign currency amount by rate.

Interest rate parity

$$\text{Future spot rate A/B} = \text{Spot rate A/B} \times \frac{1 + \text{B's interest rate}}{1 + \text{A's interest rate}}$$

Purchasing power parity

$$\text{Future spot rate A/B} = \text{Spot rate A/B} \times \frac{1 + \text{B's inflation rate}}{1 + \text{A's inflation rate}}$$

Transaction risk

is the risk of adverse exchange rate movements between the date the price is agreed and cash is received/paid, arising during normal international trade.

Netting

The process of setting off credit against debit balances so that only the net amounts are paid by currency flows. **Multilateral netting** involves offsetting several companies' balances.

Invoicing in buyer's currency

This means that the exporter bears exchange risk but may have marketing advantages/market may require invoicing in particular currency (US dollar). Exporter may be able to offset payments in foreign currency, and may be able to obtain loan on favourable terms.

Other direct risk reduction methods

- Invoicing in own currency
- Matching receipts and payments
- Lead payments (payments in advance)
- Lagged payments (delaying payments)
- Matching assets and liabilities
- Countertrade

Forward exchange contract

A firm and binding contract

For the purchase/sale of a specified quantity of a stated foreign currency

At a rate fixed at the time the contract is made

For performance at a future time agreed when contract is made

Forward rate

An exchange rate set for currencies to be exchanged at a future date.

Forward rates as adjustments to spot rates

Forward rate cheaper	–	Quoted at discount
Forward rate more expensive	–	Quoted at premium

Advantages

☑ Any amount

☑ Flexible length

Disadvantages

☒ Counterparty default

☒ Difficult to cancel

Money market hedging

Future foreign currency payment	Future foreign currency receipt
1 Borrow now in home currency	1 Borrow now in foreign currency
2 Convert home currency loan to foreign currency	2 Convert foreign currency loan to home currency
3 Put foreign currency on deposit	3 Put home currency on deposit
4 When have to make payment	4 When cash received
(a) Make payment from deposit	(a) Take cash from deposit
(b) Repay home currency borrowing	(b) Repay foreign currency borrowing

Topic List

Futures terminology

Currency futures

Currency options

Currency swaps

This chapter looks at some of the derivatives that can be used to manage financial risks, such as futures, options and swaps.

Calculations could be set on all these topics. The most important aspect here is being able to recommend the most appropriate risk management strategy.

Futures terminology

Futures contract	Obliges buyer/seller to purchase/sell specified quantity at predetermined price when contract expires
Contract size	Fixed minimum quantity of currency bought or sold using futures contract
Basis	Spot price – futures price
Basis risk	The risk that futures price movement may differ from underlying movement
Settlement date	The date when trading on a futures contract ceases and accounts are settled
Tick size	Smallest measured unit in contract price

What type of contract

Transaction on future date		Now		On future date	
Receive	currency	Sell	currency futures	Buy	currency futures
Pay	currency	Buy	currency futures	Sell	currency futures
Receive	$	Buy	currency futures	Sell	currency futures
Pay	$	Sell	currency futures	Buy	current futures

Advantages and disadvantages of futures contracts

Advantages

- Transaction costs lower than forward contracts
- Exact date of receipt or payment doesn't have to be known
- Low counterparty risk on traded markets

Disadvantages

- Can't tailor to user's exact needs
- Only available in limited number of currencies
- Hedge inefficiencies

Step 1 Setup

(a) Choose which contract (settlement date after date currency needed)

(b) Choose type of contract (buy or sell)

(c) Choose number of contracts $\dfrac{\text{Amount being hedged}}{\text{Size of contract}}$

Convert using today's futures contract price if amount being hedged is in US dollars

Step 2 Estimate closing futures price

You should be given this

Step 3 Hedge outcome

(a) **Outcome in futures market**

Opening futures price

Closing futures price

Futures profit   Movement in rate x Value of one contract x Number of contracts

(b) **Net outcome**

Spot market payment (at closing spot rate)	(X)
Futures profit/(loss) (at closing spot rate unless US company)	X
Net outcome	(X)

Currency option

A right to buy or sell currency at a stated rate of exchange at some time in the future.

Call – right to buy at fixed rate

Put – right to sell at fixed rate

Over the counter options	Tailor-made options suited to a company's specific needs.
Traded options	Contracts for standardised currency amounts, only available in certain currencies.

Choosing the right option

Complicated by lack of US dollar traded options. UK company wishing to sell US dollars can purchase £ call options (options to buy sterling with dollars).

Why option is needed

- Uncertainty about foreign currency receipts or payments (timing and amount)

- Support tender for overseas contract

- Allow publication of price lists in foreign currency

- Protect import/export of price-sensitive goods

What type of option

Transaction on future date		Now		On future date	
Receive	currency	Buy	currency put	Sell	currency
Pay	currency	Buy	currency call	Buy	currency
Receive	$	Buy	currency call	Buy	currency
Pay	$	Buy	currency put	Sell	currency

Drawbacks of options

- Cost dependent on expected volatility
- Pay on purchase
- Tailor-made options aren't negotiable
- Traded options not in every currency

Option premiums

- The exercise price
- Maturity date
- Volatility and interest rates
- Interest rate differentials

Step 1 Set up the hedge

(a) Choose contract date

(b) Decide whether put or call option required

(c) Decide which strike price applies and hence which premium

(d) Decide how many contracts, converting if necessary

(e) Calculate premium using spot rate

Step 2 Ascertain closing prices

You should be given it/them.

Step 3 Calculate outcome of hedge

(a) **Outcome in options market**

	Yes	No
Exercise?	£	£

(b) **Net outcome**

	Yes £	No £
Spot market payment (closing spot rate)	—	(X)
Option market outcome (translate balance at closing spot rate unless US company)	(X)	—
Option premium (opening spot rate unless US company)	(X)	(X)
Net outcome	(X)	(X)

Currency swaps

In a currency swap, equivalent amounts of currency are swapped for a period. However the original borrower remains liable to the lender (counterparty risk).

Risks of swaps
■ Credit risk Counterparty defaults
■ Position or market risk Unfavourable market movements
■ Political risk
■ Arrangement fees

Advantages of currency swaps

- Flexibility – any size and reversible
- Low transaction costs
- Not exposed to foreign exchange markets
- Can gain access to debt in other countries
- Restructuring currency base of liabilities
- Conversion of fixed to/from floating rate debt
- Absorb excess liquidity

Example

Edward Ltd wishes to borrow US dollars to finance an investment in America. Edward's treasurer is concerned about the high interest rates the company faces because it is not well-known in America. Edward Ltd could make an arrangement with an American company, Gordon Inc, attempting to borrow sterling in the UK money markets.

Step 1

Gordon borrows US $ and Edward borrows £. The two companies then swap funds at the current spot rate.

Step 2

Edward pays the £ interest and receives the £ interest from Gordon. Gordon pays the $ interest and receives the $ interest from Edward.

Step 3

At the end of the period the two companies swap back the principal amounts at the spot rate/predetermined rate.

13: Information strategy and systems

Topic List

Information

IS, IT and IM

Developing an information strategy

Types of information system

IT organisation

Outsourcing

In this chapter we examine information strategies and systems, starting with the need for information, and then considering the information strategy and how it is developed.

There are several types of information system such as Management Information Systems (MIS) and Decision Support Systems (DSS) you need to be aware of. Ways of evaluating information systems are also important.

The chapter concludes with how the IT department can be organised and the option of outsourcing it, which has its particular benefits and drawbacks.

Information requirements

Organisations require information for:

- **Planning:** available resources, possible timescales and likely outcomes

- **Controlling:** assessing whether activities are proceeding as planned and taking corrective action if deviations occur

- **Recording and processing transactions**

- **Performance measurement:** comparisons against budget or plan

- **Decision making:** strategic planning, management control and operational control

Strategic information

Strategic information assists strategic planning, the process of deciding on the objectives of the organisation, and planning how to achieve those objectives.

Characteristics

- Derived from internal and external sources
- Summarised at a high level
- Relevant to the long term
- Deals with whole organisation
- Often prepared on an *ad hoc* basis
- Both quantitative and qualitative

Tactical information

is used to decide how the resources of the business should be employed, and to monitor how they are and have been employed.

Characteristics

- Primarily from internal sources
- Summarised to some extent
- Relevant to the short and medium term
- Deals with activities and/or departments
- Prepared routinely and regularly
- Mainly quantitative

Operational information

is used to ensure that specific operational tasks are planned and carried out as intended. It assists in controlling day-to-day activities of the organisation.

Characteristics

- Derived entirely from internal sources
- Highly detailed
- Relates to immediate/short term
- Task-specific
- Prepared frequently, routinely
- Largely quantitative

Accurate

Complete

Cost – beneficial

User – targeted

Relevant

Authoritative

Timely

Easy to use

'Good' information is information that adds to the understanding of a situation.

Value of information

Information value depends upon:

- Its source
- Ease of assimilation
- Accessibility

Information Systems (IS)

are systems at any level of an organisation that change goals, processes, products, services or environmental relationships with the aim of gaining competitive advantage. Stratigic level IS systems are systems used by senior management for long-term decision making.

Information Technology (IT)

describes the interaction of computer technology and data transmission technology to operate systems that satisfy the organisation's information needs. These include hardware, software and operating systems.

Information Management (IM)

refers to the basic management approach to IS, including planning, environment, control, technology.

| Information | IS, IT and IM | Developing an information strategy | Types of information system | IT organisation | Outsourcing |

Information systems strategy

is the long-term plan concerned with exploiting information systems and technology, either to support business strategies or create new strategic options and competitive advantage.

The IS strategy is supported by the IT strategy and the IM strategy.

Competitive advantage

- Improve productivity and performance
- Alter management and organisational structure of business
- Lead to development of new businesses

Information technology strategy

involves deciding how information needs will be met by balancing supply and demand of funds and facilities, and the development of programmes to supply IT hardware and software.

Information management strategy

aims to ensure that information is provided to users and stored, accessed and controlled and that redundant information is not being produced.

Strategy for IS/IT

A strategy for IS/IT is justified on the grounds that it:

- Involves high costs
- Is critical to the success of many organisations
- Can be used as a source of competitive advantage
- Impacts on customer service
- Affects all levels of management
- Affects the way management information is created and presented
- Requires effective management to obtain maximum benefit
- Involves many stakeholders

Benefits of technological change

- Cuts production costs
- Develops better quality products and services
- Develops new products and services
- Provides products and services more quickly
- Frees staff from repetitive work
- Identifies markets
- Develops new distribution channels
- Removes unnecessary management
- Enhances communications with customers
- Improves management knowledge
- Enhances enterprise co-ordination

13: Information strategy and systems

| Information | IS, IT and IM | Developing an information strategy | Types of information system | IT organisation | Outsourcing |

Establishing information requirements

The identification of organisational information needs and the information framework to satisfy them is at the heart of a systems and technology strategy.

Critical success factors (CSFs)

This approach determines the information requirements of an organisation by focussing on information required to monitor and achieve those activities. An organisation will identify its CSFs when it determines its strategy:

1   List the organisation's corporate objectives and goals

2   Determine which factors are critical for accomplishing the objectives

3   Determine a small number of key performance indicators for each factor

Earl's three leg analysis

Business led

- Support for objectives
- Analytical approach
- Senior management
- Specialist teams

Infrastructure

- Operational dependence
- Evaluative approach
- Systems users
- Specialists

Mixed

- Exploit resources
- Creative approach
- Enterpreneurs

Different types of information systems serve information needs at different levels of an organisation.

Executive Information Systems (EIS) or Executive Support Systems (ESS)

EIS or ESS serve the strategic level of the organisation. They have:

- Menu driven user friendly interfaces
- Interactive graphics to help visualisation of the situation
- Communication capabilities linking the executive to external databases

An ESS summarises and tracks strategically critical information from the MIS and DSS.

Strategic Enterprise Management Systems (SEMS) and Enterprise Resource Planning Systems (ERPS)

SEMS and ERPS operate across organisational systems.

SEMS assist organisations in setting strategic goals, measuring performance, and measuring and managing intellectual capital.

ERPS handle organisational and support functions, and can link with suppliers and customers. They integrate everything into one system. They can support performance measures. ERPS should mean lower costs and investment, increased flexibility and efficiency.

Decision Support Systems (DSS) and Management Information Systems (MIS)

DSS and MIS serve middle management.

The DSS provide information, models, or tools for manipulating and/or analysing information. They support decision-making in semi-structured and unstructured situations eg, portfolio and production planning. An example of a DSS is the spreadsheet.

The MIS are used to keep records, to supply management information and to forecast. They support structured decision-making at operational and management control levels, are relatively inflexible, have an internal focus and are designed to report on existing operations.

Expert Systems

Expert system software uses a knowledge base consisting of facts, concepts and relationships and uses pattern techniques to make judgements and suggest decisions, eg on loan applications. Conditions are:

- Problem is well-defined
- Expert can define rules
- Investment is cost-justified

Expert systems are not suited to higher level, unstructured problems as these require information from a wide range of sources.

Knowledge Work Systems (KWS)

KWS help knowledge workers create and integrate knowledge into the organisation. Examples include CAD.

Office Automation Systems (OAS)

OAS create, handle and manage documents, manage workflow and scheduling, help manage client portfolios and help with communication.

Transaction Processing Systems (TPS)

TPS serve the operational level and support highly structured decisions. They are used for routine tasks where transactions must be processed so that operations can continue eg, sales order entry.

Evaluating information systems

Cost-benefit analysis

All costs and benefits must be compared, including costs of not acting. Difficult to quantify improvements in information.

Other evaluation methods

- Balanced scorecard including impact on management/structure
- Effect on competitive position
- Business case (financial/marketing/operational)
- User requirements

Technical viability

- Available technology
- Available skills
- Risk issues
- Compatibility with existing systems
- User numbers/data amounts

Operational viability

- Data availability/reliability/clarity
- Operational procedures
- Level of support/commitment
- Human resource issues
- Stakeholder impacts

Information Technology Infrastructure Library (ITIL)

ITIL provides:

- Recording and reporting on the system
- Minimising impact of adverse events
- Standard framework for change
- Minimisation of effects of systems shortcomings

IS/IT steering committee

Steering committee may oversee all developments or special projects.

Information centre

is a unit of staff with a good technical awareness of computer systems, who provide a support function to computer users within the organisation.

Delivery of IT services

- Quality of service
- Availability
- Capacity
- Continuity
- Cost-effectiveness

IT standards

The information centre is likely to be responsible for setting and encouraging users to conform to common standards.

Hardware	All organisation's equipment compatible
Software	Information easily shared
Programming	Applications follow best practice and easy to modify
Data processing	Conventions followed throughout organisation

Evaluation of IT department

- User assessment of business focus
- Degree of utilisation of support services
- Post evaluation review of implementation
- Level of participation of users
- Improvement in level of user computer literacy
- Improvement in IT staff's business awareness

The costs of the IT department may be treated as an administrative overhead, or charged out at cost or market rate.

The degree to which IT is **centralised** will depend on local needs, security and desired level of control at centre.

Outsourcing

is the use of external suppliers as a source of finished products, components or services. It is also known as **contract manufacturing** or **subcontracting**.

Types of outsourcing

- Ad-hoc
- Project management
- Partial
- Total

Outsourcing provision

Facilities management (FM)	Usually all equipment remains with the client, but the responsibility for providing and managing the specified services rests with the FM company
Timeshare	Vendor charges for access to external processing system on a time share basis
Service bureau	Concentrate on providing a specific function, eg payroll processing

Outsourcing

Advantages

- Certainly over cost
- Long-term contracts encourage planning for the future
- Economies of scale
- A specialist organisation is able to retain skills and knowledge
- New skills and knowledge become available
- Flexibility

Disadvantages

- IS may be too important to be contracted out
- Risky in commercial and/or legal terms where confidential information is available to outsiders
- Opportunities may be missed and any new technology devised by the third party could be available to competitors
- An organisation may be locked into an unsatisfactory contract
- FM does not encourage awareness of the potential costs and benefits of IS/IT

13: Information strategy and systems

Managing outsourcing arrangements

Managing outsourcing arrangements involves:

- Deciding what will be outsourced
- Choosing and negotiating with suppliers
- Managing the supplier relationship

Service level agreement

- Timescale
- Service level
- Change process
- Exit route
- Software ownership
- Dependencies
- Employment issues

Insourcing

Insourcing involves recruiting IS/IT staff internally from other areas of the business. This may be a better idea than hiring or contracting IT expertise because:

- There may not be enough qualified candidates to fill the positions available

- The cost of acquiring expertise, whether employing or outsourcing, is increasing

- The best IT professionals are people who also know and understand the business behind the systems that they develop and manage

14: Information operations

Topic List

Risks to information operations

Control framework

IT controls

Theft and fraud

Internet and e-mail

Systems development

This chapter covers the 'information operations' risks that are faced by organisations and examines the main controls used to overcome these risks. The chapter ends with systems development and the controls that should be in place to prevent systems being poorly designed and inadequately tested. This is an important chapter because questions on this area could come up frequently.

Risks to information operations

Physical damage

- Natural threats (fire, water, storms)
- Human threats (malicious, accidental)

Data and systems integrity

- Human error
- Technical error
- Data transfer
- Fraud
- Commercial espionage
- Malicious damage
- Industrial action

Internet risks

- Viruses
- Deliberate damage by employees
- Hackers
- Denial of service attacks

Other risks

- Data protection risks
- Systems development risks
- Risks to audit

Security management

Security means protection of system/information held on it from unauthorised modification, theft or destruction.

Control frameworks

CobiT framework ensures that objectives are met by providing appropriate IT systems, and linking IT processes to control objectives. CobiT provides:

- Benchmarks
- Critical success factors
- Key performance indicators

Security policy

Systematic approach to risk management covering most significant risks, control measures and contingency plans.

Management responsibilities

Top management	Establish strategy, operational responsibilities and contingency plan
User management	Establish procedures, risk assessment, controls, training
Data processing manager	Ensure applications meet security requirements
Human resources	Establish recruitment, appraisal, job rotation and division of duties

Controls over physical threats

Fire
- Site preparation eg fire proof materials
- Detection eg smoke detectors
- Extinguishers eg sprinklers
- Staff training

Water
- Waterproof ceilings and floors
- Adequate drainage

Other measures
- Physical access controls
- Good office layout
- Protected power supplies
- Separate generator
- Regular maintenance programmes

Contingency planning

A **contingency** is an unscheduled interruption of computing services that requires measures outside the day-to-day routine operating procedures.
A **contingency plan** (or **disaster recovery plan**) is a plan, formulated in advance, to be implemented upon the occurrence of certain specific future events.

Contingency plan contents

- Definition of responsibilities
- Priorities
- Backup and standby arrangements
- Communication with staff
- Public relations
- Risk assessment

Physical access controls

Physical access controls are designed to prevent intruders accessing computer equipment:

- Personnel – receptionists and security guards
- Door locks
- Keypad access system/card entry
- Intruder alarms
- Personnel identification systems

Application controls

The main controls over computer applications are:

- Input – data verification and validation
- Processing – accuracy and completeness
- Output – error reports and distribution
- Back-up – regular copies and storage off-site

Passwords

are a set of characters which may be allocated to a person, a terminal or a facility, which are required to be keyed into the system before further access is permitted to prevent unauthorised access/entry.

They enable:

- Identification of user
- Authentication of user identity
- Checks on user authority
- Restrictions of tasks/access to parts of system

Problems with passwords

- Some can be guessed easily
- Standard passwords not removed
- Users tell unauthorised persons
- Passwords left lying around

Theft

Small and portable computer equipment can easily be stolen.

Controls to mitigate theft of equipment

- Maintain equipment log
- Lock equipment away
- Site security measures

Software piracy is the unlicensed use of software by staff on an organisation's machines, or staff illegally copying software owned by the organisation.

Software piracy controls

- Buying from reputable dealers
- Maintaining purchasing and licensing records
- Maintaining central disk store
- Spot inventory checks

Fraud

Computer fraud usually involves theft of funds by dishonest use of computer.

Fraud prevention controls

- Involvement of internal audit
- Computer skills in internal audit
- Computer security policy
- Fraud awareness training
- Risk analysis
- Compliance function

The main risks arising from the internet are **viruses** and **hackers**.

Internet controls
■ Anti-virus software
■ Encryption
■ Authentication
■ Dial-back security
■ Firewalls

Intranet

is an internal network used to share information. Intranets utilise Internet technology and protocols.

E-mail

Companies should have strict policies in place over use, because of potential legal and security problems.

E-mail controls
■ Limits on personal use
■ Prohibition on defamatory/abusive material
■ Full address details and disclaimer
■ Prohibition on sending confidential information
■ Deletion of sensitive emails forbidden
■ Copying attachments to disk and check for viruses using anti-virus software

Extranet

links the intranets of related organisations, for example within a supply chain, for their mutual benefit.

Systems development life cycle

Feasibility study
Briefly review the existing system
Identify possible alternative solutions

Systems investigation
Obtain details of current requirements and user needs such as data volumes, processing cycles and timescales
Identify current problems and restrictions

Systems analysis
Consider why current methods are used and identify better alternatives

Systems design
Determine what inputs, processing and storage facilities are necessary to produce the outputs required
Consider matters such as program design, file design and security
Prepare a detailed specification of the new system
Test it

Systems implementation
Write or acquire software, test it, convert files, install hardware and start running the new system

Review and maintenance
Ensure that the new system meets current objectives, and that it continues to do so

Testing

Testing should involve:

- Systems logic
- Programs
- Overall system
- Useability and user acceptance

Staffing and training

Training will be needed when a new system is introduced, an existing system changed or new staff are recruited.

Steering committee oversees development.
Project team, including IT specialists and users, is responsible for detailed planning, design, development and implementation.

File conversion

Conversion of existing files into format suitable for new system. Possible methods:

- Direct changeover
- Parallel running
- Pilot operation
- Phased changeover

Post-implementation review

A post-implementation review should establish whether system objectives and performance criteria have been met, and if not, why not – and what should be done about it.

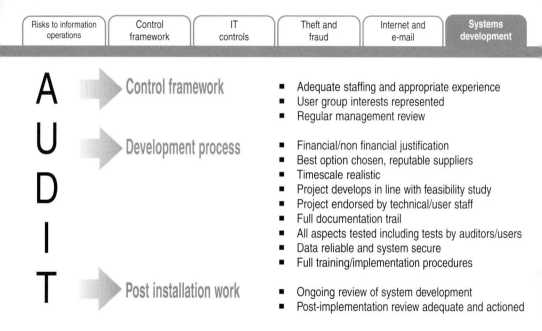

| Risks to information operations | Control framework | IT controls | Theft and fraud | Internet and e-mail | **Systems development** |

A U D I T

Control framework
- Adequate staffing and appropriate experience
- User group interests represented
- Regular management review

Development process
- Financial/non financial justification
- Best option chosen, reputable suppliers
- Timescale realistic
- Project develops in line with feasibility study
- Project endorsed by technical/user staff
- Full documentation trail
- All aspects tested including tests by auditors/users
- Data reliable and system secure
- Full training/implementation procedures

Post installation work
- Ongoing review of system development
- Post-implementation review adequate and actioned

15: Internal audit

Topic List

Role of internal audit

Internal audit assignments

Internal and external audit

Standards and ethics

Outsourcing

In this chapter, we look at the role of internal audit and the types of assignments undertaken by internal auditors. It is also important to understand the relationship between internal and external auditors. The chapter ends with a consideration of ethical aspects and standards for internal auditors.

Internal audit

is an independent appraisal function established within an organisation to examine and evaluate its activities as a service to the organisation.

Need for internal audit

Turnbull report (1999, UK) – listed companies without internal audit function should review need annually, and listed companies with internal audit should review annually its scope, authority and resources.

Need for internal audit

- Scale, diversity and complexity
- Number of employees
- Cost-benefit considerations
- Changes in organisational structure
- Changes in key risks
- Internal control problems
- Unexplained/unacceptable events

| Accounting and internal control systems | Financial and operating information | Economy, Efficiency, Effectiveness | Compliance with laws and regulations |

Objectives of internal audit

| Safeguarding of assets | Implementation of organisational objectives | Risk identification and management | Special investigations |

Transaction audits	Time consuming audits of individual transactions, used if systems have broken down or fraud is suspected
Systems audits	Audit of internal controls within the context of a system. Focus on design and operation
Risk-based audits	Assess whether responses to risks adequate, systems and processes robust and mitigate risks
Accounting systems audits	Examine operation of significant controls in major accounting areas
Computer system audits	Test security, accuracy, authorisation and back-up/contingency plan
Operational audits	Designed to confirm adequacy and implementation of control and risk management policies

Value for money audits	Focus on economy, efficiency and effectiveness in the use of resources
Best value audits	Assess whether UK local authorities are achieving continuous improvements by looking at 4Cs: Challenge, Compare, Consult, Compete
Quality audits	Review quality standards and whether actual performance meets quality standards
Management audits	Assessment of effectiveness of management and corporate structure in achievement of objectives and policies
Social audits	Coverage may include health and safety compliance, labour conditions, equal opportunities
Environmental audits	Systematic, documented, periodic and objective evaluation of how well an entity is performing in helping to safeguard the environment

External audit

is a periodic examination of the books of account and records of an entity carried out by an independent third party to ensure that they have been properly maintained, are accurate and comply with established concepts, principles, accounting standards, legal requirements and give a true and fair view of the financial state of the entity.

Distinction between internal and external audit

	Objective	Reporting	Scope	Relationship
Internal audit	Designed to add value and improve an organisation's operations.	Report to management.	Operations of the organisation.	Usually employees of the organisation, although sometimes outsourced.
External audit	Express an opinion on the financial statements.	Report to shareholders.	Financial statements.	Independent of the company and its management. They are appointed by the shareholders.

IIA Standards

Professional proficiency

This includes using staff with sufficient knowledge and experience, compliance with professional standards, proper supervision and due care.

Scope of work

Auditors should assess adequacy of controls, quality of performance, compliance with regulations and standards, asset safeguarding, VFM.

Audit performance

Proper structuring of audit work including planning, examination, reporting and follow-up.

Management

IA should have mission statement, written policies, personnel development, co-ordination with external audit and quality assurance system.

Independence and objectivity

IA should report to audit committee, not finance director and be independent of line management. Auditors should **not** audit their own work.

Outsourcing

Maintaining in-house internal audit function may be expensive and work may not justify employing full-time staff. Many organisations therefore outsource internal audit, possibly to large accountancy firms.

Using same firm to provide external and internal audit services may create independence issues and is forbidden in some jurisdictions (eg America).

Advantages of outsourcing	Disadvantages of outsourcing
☑ Provide quality staff and specialist skills	☒ Irregular monitoring of controls
☑ Assist in developing permanent internal function	☒ Greater expense as supplier makes profit
☑ Staffing and timing flexibility	☒ Frequent changes of staff
☑ More independent than employees	☒ Independence problems if same firm provides internal and external audit
☑ Better at dealing with sensitive areas	

16: Internal audit review and reporting

Topic List

Audit planning and risk analysis

Audit evidence

Audit sampling and CAATs

Analytical review

Internal audit reports

Audit committee and management review

This chapter summarises how internal audits are planned and controlled. We look at some of the tools used by internal auditors in their work, such as sampling, CAATs and analytical review.

The chapter ends with a look at internal audit reporting to the audit committee of an entity.

AUDIT PLANNING

Strategic planning

Sets out audit objectives in broad terms including:

- Areas to be covered
- Frequency of coverage
- Resource requirements

Tactical planning

Annual matching of strategic plans to resources and timetables. Includes:

- Programme
- Audit objectives
- Resource allocation
- Contingency allowance

Operational planning

Plan for each individual audit covering:

- Detailed objectives for each area
- Extent of coverage
- Target dates
- Completion arrangements
- Staff responsible

Business risks

are the risks relating to activities carried out within an entity arising from structure, systems, people, products or processes.

Assessment of business risks

Inherent risk

- Relative size of units
- Nature of transactions
- Complexity of operations
- Convertibility of assets
- Computerisation
- Reputation risks

Quality of control (control risk)

- Managerial effectiveness
- Changes in systems
- Changes in personnel
- Rapid growth
- Management pressures
- Time since last review

Risk formula

Risks can then be formally assessed using an **index** that is applied to the areas under consideration to give a ranking.

Sufficiency and appropriateness are **interrelated** & apply to both **tests of control** and **substantive** tests.

ISA 500.6

The auditor shall design and perform audit procedures that are appropriate in the circumstances for the purpose of obtaining sufficient appropriate audit evidence.

Sufficiency
Quantity

Appropriateness
Quality

External evidence (more reliable than internal)

Auditor evidence (collected from auditors better than obtained from entity)

Entity evidence (more reliable if system works well)

Written evidence (more reliable than oral)

Original evidence (original better than photocopies)

Tests of control

The auditors need evidence about two aspects of the system:

- The **design** of the systems (capable of preventing/detecting misstatements?)
- The **operation** of the systems (have they existed/operated properly in the period?)

Audit procedures
■ Inspection of assets
■ Inspection of documentation
■ Observation
■ Enquiries
■ Confirmation
■ Computations
■ Analytical procedures

Substantive tests

The auditors are seeking to **substantiate assertions** made by the directors (known as the financial statement assertions).

Financial statement assertions

Existence (an asset or liability exists at the relevant date)

Rights & obligations (asset/liability pertains to the entity at the relevant date)

Occurrence (a transaction/event took place and pertains to the entity)

Completeness (there are no items which are unrecorded or incomplete)

Valuation (asset/liability is recorded at an appropriate carrying value)

Measurement (item is recorded in the correct amount and in the right period)

Presentation/disclosure (law/standards)

Audit sampling

is the application of audit procedures to less than 100% of the items within an account balance or class of transactions such that all sampling units have a chance of selection.

Sample selection
■ Random selection
■ High value or key terms
■ All items over a certain amount
■ Items to obtain information about business
■ Items to test procedures

CAATs

are computer-assisted audit techniques, used to test controls, transactions and carry out analytical review.

Audit software

consists of computer programs used by auditors to process data of audit significance from the entity's accounting system.

Test data

is used in conducting audit procedures by entering data, such as a sample of transactions, into an entity's computer system, and comparing the results obtained with predetermined results.

Embedded audit facilities

allow a continuous review of data recorded and treated by system. Audit modules incorporated into enterprise's accounting system.

Analytical review

is an audit technique used to help analyse data to identify trends, errors, fraud, inefficiency and inconsistency. Its purpose is to understand what has happened in a system to compare this with a standard and to identify weaknesses in practice or unusual situations that may require further investigation.

Methods of analytical review

- Ratio analysis
- Non-financial performance analysis
- Internal and external benchmarking
- Trend analysis

Types of analytical procedure

Comparisons can be made with prior period information, anticipated results, predictions, industry information.

Relationships may be between different financial information that is expected to conform to a predicted pattern or between financial and non-financial information.

Ratio analysis

The analysis of relationships between different items of financial data, or financial and non-financial data.

- Comparisons required (previous periods, other companies)
- Calculation on consistent basis
- Correlation between items compared
- Greater detail strengthens analysis
- Ratios distorted by single or unusual items

Trend analysis

Analysis of changes in a given item over time, including period-by-period comparisons, weighted averages, regression analysis.

Reasonableness tests

Development of a prediction for an item based on relationships with other financial or non-financial data, eg comparison with similar firms, comparison with budgets, comparison with other financial information, credibility checks, general business review.

Audit planning and risk analysis	Audit evidence	Audit sampling and CAATs	Analytical review	**Internal audit reports**	Audit committee and management review

Recommendations for changes

Identification of risk and control issues

Ensuring action happens

REPORTING

Contents of report

- Business objectives
- Operational standards
- Risks of current practice
- Control weaknesses

- Causes of weaknesses
- Effects of weaknesses
- Recommendations to solve weaknesses

The audit committee

is a formally constituted committee of an entity's main board of directors whose responsibilities include reviewing internal financial controls, internal control and risk management systems, and monitoring the effectiveness of the internal audit function amongst others.

Benefits of audit committee

- Improve quality of financial reporting
- Create climate of control
- Enable NEDs to play positive role
- Help finance director
- Strengthen position and independence of external auditors
- Increase public confidence

Duties of audit committee

The Cadbury and Smith reports stated that the main duties were:

- **Review of financial statements** including changes in policies, judgemental areas, compliance
- **Relationship with external auditors** including appointment/removal, independence, scope, liaison
- **Review of internal audit** including standards, scope, resources, reporting, work plans, liaison with external auditors, results
- **Review of internal control** including systems adequacy, legal compliance, fraud risk, auditors' reports, disclosures
- **Review of risk management**
- **Investigations**

Review of internal controls

UK's Turnbull committee provided guidance on what board should consider:

- Risk identification/evaluation/management
- Effectiveness of internal control
- Action taken if weaknesses found

When assessing control effectiveness, consider:

- Nature and extent of risks
- Threat risks become reality
- Ability to reduce incidence/impact
- Costs and benefits of controls

Boards should receive reports covering:

- Risk and risk management
- Operation of internal controls
- Actions taken to reduce risks found
- Need for changes in control

Annual review of controls

- Changes in risks/ability to respond
- Management's monitoring of risk and control
- Extent of frequency of reports to board
- Significant controls, failures and weaknesses
- Effectiveness of public reporting

Reporting on risk management

- Acknowledgement of director responsibilities
- System provides reasonable assurance
- How directors have reviewed effectiveness
- Weaknesses leading to material losses